The
GRAVE
ROBBER

PARTICIPANT'S GUIDE

HOW JESUS CAN MAKE
YOUR IMPOSSIBLE POSSIBLE

MARK BATTERSON

BakerBooks

a division of Baker Publishing Group
Grand Rapids, Michigan

© 2014 by Mark Batterson

Published by Baker Books
a division of Baker Publishing Group
P.O. Box 6287, Grand Rapids, MI 49516-6287
www.bakerbooks.com

Printed in the United States of America

Library of Congress Cataloging-in-Publication Data
Batterson, Mark.
    The grave robber participant's guide : how Jesus can make your impossible possible / Mark Batterson.
      pages cm
    Includes bibliographical references.
    ISBN 978-0-8010-1596-0 (pbk.)
    1. Bible. John—Criticism, interpretation, etc.—Textbooks. 2. Miracles—Biblical teaching—Textbooks. I. Title.
    BS2615.6.M5B383 2014
    226.7'06—dc23   2014020858

The author is represented by Fedd & Company, Inc.

15 16 17 18 19 20   7 6 5 4

CONTENTS

INTRODUCTION

Thirty-four distinct miracles are recorded in the Gospels, while countless more went unrecorded. John's Gospel spotlights seven miracles, unveiling seven dimensions of Jesus' miraculous power. Like the sun rising in the east, each miracle reveals another ray of God's glory until Lazarus steps out of the shadow of his tomb and into the light of the Grave Robber.

Maybe you're at a place in your life where you need a miracle. Don't we all at some point in our lives? And God wants to do *now* what He did *then*. But this is more than a course in miracles. It's a study about the only One who can perform them. The seven miracles are seven signs, and each sign points straight to Jesus. So let me offer a word of caution at the outset:

Don't seek miracles.
Follow Jesus.
And if you follow Jesus long enough and far enough, you'll eventually find yourself in the middle of some miracles.

Everyone wants a miracle. But here's the catch: no one wants to be in a situation that necessitates one! Of course, you can't have one without the other. The prerequisite for a miracle is a problem, and the bigger the problem, the greater the potential miracle. If the wedding party in Cana hadn't run out of wine, there would have been no need for the Wine Maker to do what He did. What the bride and groom perceived as a problem was really a perfect opportunity for God to reveal His glory. And nothing has changed since Jesus turned water into wine, healed a man born blind, or called Lazarus out of his tomb four days after his funeral.

He is the God who can make your impossible possible!

THE FIRST SIGN

WATER INTO WINE

Before watching Session 1 of the *Grave Robber* DVD,
read chapters 1–6 in *The Grave Robber*.

Read, pray, and meditate on the first sign, found in John 2:1–10:

On the third day a wedding took place at Cana in Galilee. Jesus' mother was there, and Jesus and his disciples had also been invited to the wedding. When the wine was gone, Jesus' mother said to him, "They have no more wine."

"Woman, why do you involve me?" Jesus replied. "My hour has not yet come."

His mother said to the servants, "Do whatever he tells you."

Nearby stood six stone water jars, the kind used by the Jews for ceremonial washing, each holding from twenty to thirty gallons.

Jesus said to the servants, "Fill the jars with water"; so they filled them to the brim.

Then he told them, "Now draw some out and take it to the master of the banquet."

They did so, and the master of the banquet tasted the water that had been turned into wine. He did not realize where it had come from, though the servants who had drawn the water knew. Then he called the bridegroom aside and said, "Everyone brings out the choice wine first and then the cheaper wine after the guests have had too much to drink; but you have saved the best till now."

Write down your personal reflections.

_____

_____

_____

_____

_____

_____

_____

_____

_____

Introduction

For nearly thirty years, the One who had crafted the universe with His voice crafted furniture with His hands. And He was good at what He did—no crooked table legs ever came out of the carpenter's shop in Nazareth.[1] But Jesus was more than a master carpenter. He was also God incognito. For three decades, His miracles were history's best-kept secret. But that all changed the day water blushed in the face of its Creator.

Thirty-four distinct miracles are recorded in the Gospels. But John's Gospel spotlights seven of them. It's those seven miracles that we're going to explore during this study of _The Grave Robber_. And it all begins in Cana.

This is where Jesus turned water into wine.

This is where the cabinetmaker became the Wine Maker.

Video Notes

As you watch the video for this session, use the following space to take notes.

_____

_____

_____

_____

_____

_____

_____

_____

_____

_____

_____

_____

_____

_____

_____

Group Discussion

1. In the introduction to the *Grave Robber* study, there is a caution not to seek miracles but rather to seek Jesus. Has there ever been a time in your life when you were seeking a miracle more than you were seeking Jesus? Perhaps you sought God for the *right thing* in the *wrong way*, at the *wrong time*, or for the *wrong reason*. Share your experience and what you learned from it with the group.

2. We all want a miracle, but none of us wants to be in a situation that necessitates one. Of course, you can't have one without the other. Share with the group a situation in *your past* or *your present* when you needed God to do a miracle.

3. Oliver Wendell Holmes once said that once the mind is stretched by a new idea, it never returns to its original dimensions.[2] The goal of this study is to not only stretch your mind but also stretch your faith. Share with the group an experience that stretched your faith to new dimensions. What happened? What did you learn from it? And how do you believe God wants to stretch your faith through this study?

4. This first miracle isn't about saving a life. It's about saving face. It reveals how much God cares about the minute details of our lives. God is great not just because nothing is too *big*. God is great because nothing is too *small*.

> Matthew 10:29–31 says:
>
>> Are not two sparrows sold for a penny? Yet not one of them will fall to the ground outside your Father's care. And even the very hairs of your head are all numbered. So don't be afraid; you are worth more than many sparrows.

How has God demonstrated His greatness in the small details of your life? Do you find it easier to trust God for the big things, like keeping the planets in orbit, or the small things, like your financial problems or emotional issues?

5. The first miracle reveals God's mastery and majesty at a molecular level. Is there a microscopic issue in your life where you need to trust God more? A negative situation at work that you cannot seem to change? A small problem that could become a major relational issue if you don't deal with it? A dream that is beyond your ability or beyond your resources?

Final Thoughts

One of the boldest statements in the Bible is John 14:12:

> Whoever believes in me will do the works I have been doing, and they will do even greater things than these.

What do you think Jesus meant by "greater things"?
How is that evidenced in the rest of the New Testament?
What does that mean for your life?

If you follow Jesus, you'll do what He did. You'll seek to please the heavenly Father first and foremost. You'll care for the poor, you'll wash feet, and you'll undoubtedly offend some Pharisees along the way. But you'll also traffic in the miraculous. Make no mistake about it: *only God can perform miracles*. So God gets all of the glory. But nearly every miracle has a human element. You've got to do the natural before God will do the supernatural.

Is there a *natural* step you need to take before God will do the *supernatural*?

Reflection Questions

1. If you don't know what you want to get out of this *Grave Robber* study, you probably won't get much out of it. Take a few minutes to identify where God wants to stretch you. Is it a dream that is beyond your resources? A problem that is beyond your ability to solve? A situation that is beyond your ability to resolve? Write down the top three things you want to get out of this study.

1. _____

   _____

   _____

   _____

2. _____

   _____

   _____

   _____

3. _____

   _____

   _____

   _____

2. On a scale of 1 to 10, how easy or hard is it for you to believe in miracles?

1	2	3	4	5	6	7	8	9	10
Easy									**Hard**

3. Trust isn't measured by word count. In fact, the more trust you have, the fewer words you need. How does your lack of trust get expressed?

_____

_____

_____

_____

_____

4. Nearly every miracle has a human element. You've got to do the natural before God will do the supernatural. What do you need to do to position yourself for the supernatural? What step do you need to take?

_____

_____

_____

5. The single greatest miracle is the forgiveness of sin made possible through the crucifixion and resurrection of the sinless Son of God. There is no close second. That

miracle is available to anyone, anytime but the miracle of salvation isn't the finish line. It's the baseline.

Have you experienced the miracle of forgiveness? If so, thank God once again for the greatest of miracles. If not, you can experience that miracle right here, right now. It's as simple as confessing your sin and professing your faith in Jesus Christ. Now tell a friend or leader in your group about the decision you've made.

The Next Step

The catalyst for the first miracle was Mary nudging Jesus, as only a mother can. She perceived the problem—running out of wine—as an opportunity. And she simply said, "They have no more wine."[3]

Is there someone in your life who finds themselves in the middle of a problem they cannot solve? Maybe it's an opportunity for you to speak a word of encouragement, offer to help them out financially, or begin to circle their problem in prayer.

Remember, *you are someone else's miracle*. Who is that person?

As the Holy Spirit prompts you, look for opportunities to be someone else's miracle. Don't try to manufacture a miracle. Simply make yourself available to the Holy Spirit's nudges.

Make a list of people you are going to pray for during this seven-week study.

1. _____

2. _____

3. _____

THE SECOND SIGN

SUPERNATURAL SYNCHRONICITIES

Before watching Session 2,
read chapters 7–9 in *The Grave Robber*.

Read, pray, and meditate on the second sign, found in John 4:46–54:

Once more he visited Cana in Galilee, where he had turned the water into wine. And there was a certain royal official whose son lay sick at Capernaum. When this man heard that Jesus had arrived in Galilee from Judea, he went to him and begged him to come and heal his son, who was close to death.

"Unless you people see signs and wonders," Jesus told him, "you will never believe."

The royal official said, "Sir, come down before my child dies."

"Go," Jesus replied, "your son will live."

The man took Jesus at his word and departed. While he was still on the way, his servants met him with the news that his boy was living. When he inquired as to the time when his son got better, they said to him, "Yesterday, at one in the afternoon, the fever left him."

Then the father realized that this was the exact time at which Jesus had said to him, "Your son will live." So he and his whole household believed.

This was the second sign Jesus performed after coming from Judea to Galilee.

Write down your personal reflections.

_____

_____

_____

_____

_____

_____

_____

_____

Introduction

Jesus wasn't moved by "religious correctness"—if He had been, He would have called the Pharisees to be His followers. But He was nonplussed by their show of religion. Jesus was moved by desperate people who took desperate measures to get to Him. When a tax collector named Zacchaeus climbed a tree to get a glimpse of Jesus, Jesus reciprocated by inviting him to lunch.

The royal official was desperate because of his son's high fever. So he defied the social order of his day and sought an audience with a Jewish rabbi. He was willing to humble himself before someone he had political power over. And Jesus reciprocated by healing his son.

If you want God to do something new in your life, you can't keep doing the same old thing. You have to do something different. You may have to walk all the way from Capernaum to Cana, but you'll never regret one second of time, one ounce of energy, or one penny of money invested in seeking Jesus.

It won't just save your life.

It will save your soul.

Video Notes

As you watch the video for this session, use the following space to take notes.

_____

_____

_____

_____

_____

_____

_____

_____

Group Discussion

1. The video teaching begins with a benediction coined by Dr. Richard Halverson:

   > You go nowhere by accident.
   >
   > Wherever you go, God is sending you.
   >
   > Wherever you are, God has put you there.

   Share with the group a time when you found yourself in a place you didn't want to be but later discovered it was precisely where you needed to be. What lesson did God teach you through that experience?

2. One way God expresses His sovereignty is by strategically positioning us in the right place at the right time. Have you ever met the *right* person at the *right* place at the *right* time, and the only explanation was God? Share it with the group.

3. Who is the royal official in your life? Is there someone who seems to be "out of your league"? Someone you

have no business doing business with? Someone you'd like to meet but have no idea how? With God, there is only one degree of separation between you and everybody else on the planet, because you know God and God knows everybody! If you feel comfortable, share the name or share the situation with the group. Now take a few minutes to specifically pray for divine appointments for one another. As God answers those prayers over the course of this study, share them with the group.

4. The video teaching details the calories burned between Capernaum and Cana. Mark also shares about his Half Dome hike. What's the most difficult thing you've ever done? The most calories you've burned in a single day? What do you think would happen if you put that same kind of effort into seeking Jesus?

5. The second miracle reveals God's mastery over time and space. Is there a situation in your life where you need to trust God for a long-distance miracle? A situation you can't control? A situation you can't change? Are you willing to go out of your way to see God intervene? Share

with the group a way that you need to inconvenience yourself this week.

Final Thoughts

Many people who think they are following Jesus have actually invited Jesus to follow them. They invert the gospel. They want God to serve their purposes, not the other way around. But the true spiritual adventure begins when you follow Jesus—wherever, whenever.

Most of us follow Jesus to the point of inconvenience but no further. We're more than willing to follow Jesus as long as it doesn't detour our plans. But it was the willingness to be inconvenienced that defined the Good Samaritan. And that's how he became someone else's miracle. Most miracles don't happen on Main Street. They happen off the beaten path, about twenty miles out of town.

When was the last time you inconvenienced yourself to help someone?

Where do you need to be inconvenienced in your relationship with God?

Don't settle for the path of least resistance.

Take the road less traveled.

Reflection Questions

Whether you're taking a trip to the grocery store or a mission trip halfway around the world, God is setting up divine appointments along the way. The challenge, of course, is that they are often harder to recognize closer to home. We're so busy doing what we have to do and getting where we have to go that we sometimes miss the miracles that are right in front of us.

1. On a scale of 1 to 10, how good are you at recognizing divine appointments?

1	2	3	4	5	6	7	8	9	10
Not So Good									Good

   How can you become more intentional about seizing divine appointments? Maybe it's initiating a conversation with a neighbor or co-worker whom you usually ignore. Maybe it's offering a helping hand to someone who needs it when you have very little time or energy left. What are some steps you are going to take to better position yourself for the miraculous?

_____

_____

_____

2. The royal official marked this moment. He specifically noted that it was the seventh hour or one o'clock in the afternoon. One way to mark moments is the discipline of journaling. It's the way we make a paper trail of God's faithfulness.

Second Corinthians 10:5 says, "Take captive every thought to make it obedient to Christ." One of the best ways to take thoughts captive is to write them down. After all, the shortest pencil is longer than the longest memory! If you don't keep a journal, go out and buy one. Start marking moments—things you're grateful for, things you're praying for. Writing them down will help you remember to give God the glory He deserves when your prayers are answered.

Start by making a prayer list for this week:

1. _____

2. _____

3. _____

3. If you want to experience the miraculous, you need to make every effort to get in close proximity to the healing power of Jesus. That's what the woman with the issue of blood did. She fought through the crowds to touch the hem of His garment. That's what the woman with the alabaster jar of perfume did. She crashed a party at a Pharisee's house. That's what the four friends of an invalid did. They airlifted their friend through a hole in the ceiling.

Take a few minutes to read and reflect on those stories in Luke 8:43–48; Luke 7:36–50; and Mark 2:1–12.

What is the common denominator between the stories? How can you follow suit?

_____

_____

_____

_____

What steps did they take?

_____

_____

_____

_____

_____

_____

_____

_____

4. Loving God with all of your strength means expending energy for kingdom causes. It's how you get sweat equity in the kingdom of God. How can you break a sweat or burn some calories for the kingdom this week?

_____

_____

_____

_____

The Next Step

Go back to Cana.

The second miracle Jesus performed happened in the same place as the first miracle. And that is no coincidence. It's easier to believe God for a miracle in a place where you've experienced one before. For me, that's the rooftop of Ebenezer's coffeehouse. I have more faith when I'm praying on top of a miracle God has already done.

What is your Ebenezer's coffeehouse?

What is your Cana?

For Moses, it was a burning bush on the back side of the desert.

For David, it was the Valley of Elah, where he defeated Goliath.

For Elijah, it was Mount Carmel, where he defeated the prophets of Baal.

For Peter, it was the Sea of Galilee, where he walked on water.

And for Paul, it was the road to Damascus.

Where is your Cana?

What did God do there?

Maybe it's time to revisit Cana to renew your faith.

THE THIRD SIGN

VERY SUPERSTITIOUS

Before watching Session 3,
read chapters 10–12 in *The Grave Robber*.

Read, pray, and meditate on the third sign, found in John 5:1–9:

> Some time later, Jesus went up to Jerusalem for one of the Jewish festivals. Now there is in Jerusalem near the Sheep Gate a pool, which in Aramaic is called Bethesda and which is surrounded by five covered colonnades. Here a great number of disabled people used to lie—the blind, the lame, the paralyzed. One who was there had been an invalid for thirty-eight years. When Jesus saw him lying there and learned that he had been in this condition for a long time, he asked him, "Do you want to get well?"
>
> "Sir," the invalid replied, "I have no one to help me into the pool when the water is stirred. While I am trying to get in, someone else goes down ahead of me."
>
> Then Jesus said to him, "Get up! Pick up your mat and walk." At once the man was cured; he picked up his mat and walked.

Write down your personal reflections.

God is always able to do
anything.
  Do not label anyone - Apple + child
of God.

_____

_____

_____

_____

_____

_____

_____

_____

Introduction

In *The Grave Robber*, Mark details the true story of George Dantzig, a graduate student at the University of California who made a remarkable breakthrough in mathematics. George was late to class one day in 1939, missing the professor's disclaimer that the two problems on the blackboard were two of statistics' unsolvable problems. George thought they were the homework assignment. While it took longer than normal and was much harder than the typical assignment, George Dantzig managed to solve both problems. George later commented, "If someone had told me they were two famous unsolved problems, I probably wouldn't have even tried to solve them."[4]

And therein lies our problem.

We have not because we ask not.
We have not because we try not.
We have not because we believe not.

We make far too many false assumptions about what *is* and what *isn't* possible. The biblical reality is that we can do *all things* through Christ who strengthens us.[5] We live in an alternate reality where all things are possible. Why? Because God is able to do immeasurably more than all we can ask or imagine according to His power that is at work within us.[6]

Video Notes

As you watch the video for this session, use the following space to take notes.

_____

_____

_____

_____

_____

SESSION 3

Group Discussion

1. Are there any assumptions you made as a kid that you were surprised to find out weren't really true?

2. It's never too late to be who you might have been. Are there any parts of your personality or seasons of your life that you feel the enemy has stolen? God wants to redeem them, to restore them. He doesn't just want to give them back. He wants to give them back with interest.

   Read Joel 2:21–27. Take special note of the promise in verse 25: "I will repay you for the years the locusts have eaten."

   Share a redemption story from your life.

3. To the infinite all finites are equal. To an omnipotent God, there is no big or small, easy or difficult, possible or impossible. Luke 1:37 says, "Nothing is impossible with God" (NLT). Then, in Matthew 19:26, Jesus said, "With God, all things are possible." Why do you think the Bible says the same thing two ways?

4. Have you ever been in a situation where you couldn't help someone because they didn't want help? How did you handle it? What can you learn from the story in John 9 about how to deal with that kind of situation? Don't just share the story with the group; pray for that person or that situation.

5. The video teaching says, "If you want to experience the miraculous, you need to unlearn every assumption you've ever made, except for one: God is able!" What false assumptions have you been made aware of during this *Grave Robber* study?

Final Thoughts

The story of God delivering on His promise to Abraham and Sarah is a quick and easy read. It takes only a few minutes to get from promise to fulfillment. But those *twenty-five years* of waiting had to feel like an eternity to Abraham and Sarah.

Yet they held out hope. In fact, Romans 4:17 says, "Against all hope, Abraham in hope believed."

Is there a situation in your life where you need to not just hope, but *hope against hope*? Take heart. The invalid held out hope for thirty-eight years! There is no statute of limitations on God's promises. Second Corinthians 1:20 says, "No matter how many promises God has made, they are 'Yes' in Christ."

And they aren't just *yes*.

They are *yes* and *amen*.

Reflection Questions

1. One of the key takeaways from this session is this: *don't let what's wrong with you define you*. But that's easier said than done, and not only in the way we see ourselves but also in the way we see others. The Pharisees tended to judge people based on what they had done wrong—past tense. Jesus saw people's potential. How do you see people? Are there any labels that have been placed on you that you need to rebuke in Jesus' name?

_____

_____

2. On a scale of 1 to 10, how do you tend to see people?

1	2	3	4	5	6	7	8	9	10
Past Mistakes									**Future Potential**

3. It's easy to become accustomed to our crutches. Or in the case of the invalid, adjusted to our two-foot-by-four-foot mat. That mat doubled as his security blanket. What is your two-foot-by-four-foot mat? What is your security blanket? What crutch do you need to get rid of?

_____

_____

_____

4. Do you want to get well? Until the pain of staying the same is greater than the pain of change, most problems get worse. What short-term pain do you need to endure for the sake of long-term gain?

_____

_____

_____

5. The video teaching talks about getting a second opinion from the Great Physician. The Bible is that second opinion. It's more than a diagnosis. It's also a prognosis. Identify three promises you need to circle, need to stand on, need to claim this coming week.

1. _____

2. _____

3. _____

The Next Step

Our culture has a tendency to reduce people to labels. Not only is that unhealthy and unholy, but it's also dehumanizing. Don't let anyone label you besides the One who made you. Here's what the Bible says:

You are *more than a conqueror.*[7]
You are *the apple of God's eye.*[8]
You are *sought after.*[9]
You are *a joint heir with Christ.*[10]
You are *a child of God.*[11]

The Bible is a mirror that enables us to see ourselves for who we really are. But you can't just take an occasional glance. You need to stare at it until it changes the reflection you see in the mirror.

The Bible wasn't just meant to be *read*.

It was meant to be *meditated on*.

This coming week, meditate on the five dimensions of your identity listed above, or come up with your own list. Let those new labels replace the old labels that others have placed on your life.

THE FOURTH SIGN

TWO FISH

Before watching Session 4,
read chapters 13–15 in *The Grave Robber*.

Read, pray, and meditate on the fourth sign, found in John 6:1–13.

Some time after this, Jesus crossed to the far shore of the Sea of Galilee and a great crowd of people followed him because they saw the signs he had performed by healing the sick. Then Jesus went up on a mountainside and sat down with his disciples. The Jewish Passover Festival was near.

When Jesus looked up and saw a great crowd coming toward him, he said to Philip, "Where shall we buy bread for these people to eat?" He asked this only to test him, for he already had in mind what he was going to do.

Philip answered him, "It would take more than half a year's wages to buy enough bread for each one to have a bite!"

Another of his disciples, Andrew, Simon Peter's brother, spoke up, "Here is a boy with five small barley loaves and two small fish, but how far will they go among so many?"

Jesus said, "Have the people sit down." There was plenty of grass in that place, and they sat down (about five thousand men were there). Jesus then took the loaves, gave thanks, and distributed to those who were seated as much as they wanted. He did the same with the fish.

When they had all had enough to eat, he said to his disciples, "Gather the pieces that are left over. Let nothing be wasted." So they gathered them and filled twelve baskets with the pieces of the five barley loaves left over by those who had eaten.

Write down your personal reflections.

_____

_____

_____

_____

_____

_____

_____

_____

Introduction

Chapter 13 of *The Grave Robber* spotlights a study done by researchers at Carnegie Mellon University.[12] It was devised to discover why people respond to the needs of others. One group of participants received a charity request letter that featured statistics about the magnitude of the problems facing children in Africa. The second group received a letter focused on the needs of one seven-year-old girl named Rokia.

On average, the participants who read the statistical letter contributed $1.14.

The people who read about Rokia gave $2.38—more than twice as much.

The smaller donations in response to the statistical letter were the result of something psychologists call the "drop in the bucket effect." If we feel overwhelmed by the scale of the problem, we often don't do anything about it because we don't think we can make a difference. Statistics can actually make us *less* charitable! Statistics can short-circuit a compassionate response by shifting people into an analytical frame of mind. And thinking analytically can hinder people's ability to act compassionately. The head gets in the way of the heart. The researchers came to this conclusion: the mere act of calculation reduces compassion.

It reduces miracles too!

Video Notes

As you watch the video for this session, use the following space to take notes.

_____

_____

_____

_____

Group Discussion

1. What's your all-time favorite food? Order a case of Malnati's pizza for your next group session or plan a group outing to someone's favorite restaurant to enjoy a night of food and fellowship.

2. Have you ever found yourself in a situation where enough wasn't enough but God made miraculous provision? Share it with the group.

3. What do you do when you know God wants you to take a job that pays less, but you won't be able to pay off your school loans? When you know God wants you to go on the mission trip, but you can't afford the days off? When you know God wants you to adopt a child or go to grad school or give to a kingdom cause, but it just doesn't fit in your budget? Have you ever found yourself in a place where the will of God just didn't add up? What did you do?

4. The act of giving thanks is the precursor to many a miracle in Scripture, including the multiplication of the five loaves and two fish. Is there something you need to praise God for that has not happened yet? Pause to spend some time praising God—giving thanks for what God *has done* and *will do*.

5. In God's economy, 5 + 2 doesn't equal 7. Actually, 5 + 2 = 5,000 R12. The disciples had more left over than they started with. This was an "only God" moment. Have you ever had one of those "only God" moments? Share it with the group.

Final Thoughts

Any time you *add* something to the gospel, you actually *subtract* from it. That is certainly true of the prosperity gospel, as detailed in *The Grave Robber*. The goal of giving is not a material blessing. The goal is storing up treasures in heaven.

But God does not default on His promises. And the reality is this: *you cannot out-give God.*

In the words of Jesus in Luke 6:38, "Give, and it will be given to you. A good measure, pressed down, shaken together and running over, will be poured into your lap. For with the measure you use, it will be measured to you."

The law of measures is as inviolable as the law of gravity!

With the measure you use, it will be measured unto you. It doesn't matter whether it's two fish or two mites, you can take it to the bank. You cannot break the law of measures, and that's good news if you give your brown bag lunch to Jesus.

Reflection Questions

1. The lesson of the fourth miracle is simple: if you put what you have in your hands into God's hands, He can make a lot out of a little! If you have a scarcity mentality, you'll hang on to what you have. Why? Because the more you give, the less you'll have. The abundance mentality is the exact opposite: the more you give away, the more God can give back. Where are you on the scarcity to abundance scale?

1	2	3	4	5	6	7	8	9	10
Scarcity									Abundance

2. What do you do when the will of God doesn't add up? Do you default to logic? Or do you believe that God will multiply? Read Numbers 11. Write your reflections below.

_____

_____

_____

_____

_____

3. Your job is not to crunch numbers and audit the will of God. After all, the will of God is not a zero-sum game. When you add God to the equation, two fish can go a lot further than you imagine. What are the "two fish" you need to give to God?

_____

_____

_____

_____

_____

_____

4. Before the miracle of multiplication, Jesus gave thanks. That simple act of gratitude set up this miracle. If you don't keep a gratitude journal, start one. If you already do, start numbering your entries. It's a practical way to "count your blessings." Start your list here.

_____

_____

_____

_____

_____

5. Nothing is too big for God. Jeremiah 32:17 says it this way: "Ah, Sovereign LORD, you have made the heavens and the earth by your great power and outstretched arm. Nothing is too hard for you." We have a tendency to ask God to do things that are just outside our ability. Is there an impossible situation in your life that "only God" can solve? An impossible person? An impossible dream? Write it down and start believing that God is bigger than your biggest mistakes, biggest fears, biggest dreams.

_____

_____

_____

The Next Step

The stories of the financial faith of George Müller and John Wesley are profiled in *The Grave Robber*, along with testimonies of God's provision for National Community Church. God wants to write a similar story through you. He wants to multiply His blessings in your life, but not so you can spend it selfishly on yourself. Jesus didn't die so you can wear nicer clothes or drive a nicer car. He does, however, want to bless you so that you can be a bigger blessing to others! You are blessed to bless.

If you've never played "The Giving Game," why not start this week?

Pay a visit to http://theaterchurch.com/media/featured/i-like-home and watch *I Like Home*, a story that profiles how one couple leveraged their home to bless someone who was homeless.

As you watch that video and other giving stories at www.ilikegiving.com, pray for opportunities to be a blessing to someone this week.

Be prepared to share that giving story with the group next week.

THE FIFTH SIGN

WALKING ON WATER

Before watching Session 5,
read chapters 16–18 in *The Grave Robber*.

Read, pray, and meditate on the fifth sign, found in John 6:16–21:

> When evening came, his disciples went down to the lake, where they got into a boat and set off across the lake for Capernaum. By now it was dark, and Jesus had not yet joined them. A strong wind was blowing and the waters grew rough. When they had rowed about three or four miles, they saw Jesus approaching the boat, walking on the water; and they were frightened. But he said to them, "It is I; don't be afraid." Then they were willing to take him into the boat, and immediately the boat reached the shore where they were heading.

Write down your personal reflections.

_____

_____

_____

_____

_____

_____

Introduction

Walking.

It's something most of us take for granted, but not Casey and Theresa. When their daughter, Lily Kate, was four months of age, an ultrasound showed abnormal brain development. She was diagnosed with a rare brain malformation that doctors told them would affect her mental and motor development. Shortly thereafter, Lily Kate experienced her first seizure.

"No, she's not walking yet." The pain of saying that statement over and over was excruciating for Casey and Theresa. But they refused to give up hope. They have fought for their daughter, both through prayer and through therapy. They've also learned to find good and find God in little triumphs. They find hope in each smile, each laugh, each day, each developmental progression. In Theresa's words, "Perhaps our miracle isn't going to be seen medically. Maybe it will be seen in the daily overcoming—as we look at our amazing and courageous girl, wondering how in the world she keeps moving forward amidst the challenges of her circumstances."[13]

At two years of age, against all odds, Lily Kate took her first steps. It took longer and it was much harder than for a child without Lily's condition. But maybe that's all the more reason to rejoice.

No matter what challenges you face, every miracle begins with the first step. You need to step out, step up. But if you have the courage to take one small step, the Water Walker can turn it into a giant leap forward.

Video Notes

As you watch the video for this session, use the following space to take notes.

Group Discussion

1. Most miracles are preceded by a scary step of faith. Have you ever felt like you were stepping out of the boat and onto the water?

2. In God's kingdom, playing it safe is risky. Take a moment to read and reflect on the parable of the talents in Matthew 25:14–30. The servant who played it safe by burying his talent had it taken away from him. In fact, Jesus called him *wicked*. Why do you think Jesus used such strong language?

3. In the video teaching, Mark shared one of the scariest moments from his childhood. Share a scary moment with the group. How did it impact you?

4. Matthew's Gospel says the disciples were "beaten by the waves" (14:24 ESV). In other words, they were fighting a losing battle. Have you ever felt that way? How did you persevere? If you feel that way now, let the group pause and pray for perseverance for you.

5. What is your greatest fear? The fear of failure? The fear of rejection? Fear of the future?

Final Thoughts

As Mark Nepo said, "Birds don't need ornithologists to fly."[14] But there comes a moment when we need someone to push us out of the nest or call us out of the boat. That's what Jesus did with Peter—he called him out. Is there someone in your life who you need to call out of their complacency? Don't be afraid to speak the truth in love.

Indecision is a decision.
Inaction is an action.

There is nothing wrong with thinking through or praying through a situation. But don't overthink it. There comes a point when you don't need more facts.

What you need is more faith.

Reflection Questions

1. Most miracles don't happen within sight of the shoreline. You have to row about thirty furlongs out to sea. You have to sail away from shore. You have to sail into fear. That's what Paul did when he returned to Jerusalem. He was actually warned not to come back. But Paul says in Acts 20:22–23: "And now, compelled by the Spirit, I am going to Jerusalem, not knowing what will happen to me there. I only know that in every city the Holy Spirit warns me that prison and hardships are facing me." Does God call us into danger? Is it possible that imprisonment or affliction is part of God's plan? Take a few moments to reflect and journal your answer.

_____

_____

_____

_____

_____

2. Some people seem to be natural risk takers. They have a high threshold for high-stakes risks. Others seem to be risk averse. Where would you rank yourself on the risk scale?

1	2	3	4	5	6	7	8	9	10
Low Threshold							**High Threshold**		

3. The key to overcoming the fear of failure isn't success. It's failure in small enough doses that you build up an immunity to fear. You discover that failure isn't the end of the world. You discover that God is right there to pick you back up again. What are your greatest fears? How have you or how can you build up an immunity to them?

_____

_____

_____

4. We don't need to know more. We need to do more with what we know. Or to put it another way: we don't need more facts; we need more faith. Where and how is God stretching your faith?

_____

_____

5. If you're going to get out of a boat in the middle of the Sea of Galilee in the middle of the night, you had better make sure Jesus said, "Come." Of course, if Jesus says, "Come," you had better not stay in the boat. Is there a boat you need to get out of?

The Next Step

If you want to walk on water, you have to get out of the boat.

It's that simple.
It's that difficult.

I don't remember who said it or where I heard it, but it's always been one of my favorite definitions of faith: *faith is climbing out on a limb, cutting it off, and watching the tree fall*. For Lora and me, it was our cross-country move to Washington, DC. We didn't just climb out on the limb. We cut it off.

What limb do you need to cut off?

We often want God to reveal the second step before we take the first step, but faith is often taking the first step without knowing where it will lead. That's what Abraham did, isn't it?

Hebrews 11:8 says, "By faith Abraham, when called to go to a place he would later receive as his inheritance, obeyed and went, even though he did not know where he was going."

Don't worry about the second step, or third step, or one hundredth step.

What's the *next step* you need to take?

Take a concrete step in that direction this week.

Who knows? That one small step could prove to be a giant leap in your life.

THE SIXTH SIGN

NEVER SAY NEVER

Before watching Session 6,
read chapters 19–21 in *The Grave Robber*.

Read, pray, and meditate on the sixth sign, found in John 9:1–11:

As he went along, he saw a man blind from birth. His disciples asked him, "Rabbi, who sinned, this man or his parents, that he was born blind?"

"Neither this man nor his parents sinned," said Jesus, "but this happened so that the works of God might be displayed in him. As long as it is day, we must do the works of him who sent me. Night is coming, when no one can work. While I am in the world, I am the light of the world."

After saying this, he spit on the ground, made some mud with the saliva, and put it on the man's eyes. "Go," he told him, "wash in the Pool of Siloam" (this word means "Sent"). So the man went and washed, and came home seeing.

His neighbors and those who had formerly seen him begging asked, "Isn't this the same man who used to sit and beg?" Some claimed that he was.

Others said, "No, he only looks like him."

But he himself insisted, "I am the man."

"How then were your eyes opened?" they asked.

He replied, "The man they call Jesus made some mud and put it on my eyes. He told me to go to Siloam and wash. So I went and washed, and then I could see."

Write down your personal reflections.

_____

_____

_____

_____

_____

_____

_____

_____

_____

Introduction

Every *ology* is a branch of theology.

Whether they know it or not, the astronomer who charts the stars, the geneticist who maps the genome, the oceanographer who explores the barrier reef, the ornithologist who studies and preserves rare bird species, the physicist who tries to catch quarks, and the chemist who synthesizes chemical compounds into pharmaceutical drugs are all indirectly studying the Creator by studying His creation.

While Scripture belongs in a category by itself as special revelation, God has revealed different facets of who He is through nature. And if you turn a blind eye to natural revelation, special revelation isn't as special. Albert Einstein said it best: "Science without religion is lame, and conversely, religion without science is blind."[15]

So while science is a poor substitute for Scripture, it makes a wonderful complement to it. In fact, some miracles don't make sense without it, and the sixth miracle is one of them. Jesus doesn't just heal blind eyes. He rewires a blind man's brain. This is nothing short of synaptogenesis.

Video Notes

As you watch the video for this session, use the following space to take notes.

_____

_____

_____

_____

_____

_____

_____

_____

_____

_____

_____

_____

_____

_____

_____

_____

_____

Group Discussion

1. What comes to mind when you hear the word *lake*, *car*, or *pet*?

2. Why didn't Jesus just heal this man on the spot? Why send him on a scavenger hunt?

3. Have you ever tried to manufacture a miracle? What did you do? What did you learn from the experience?

4. God's forgiveness is bigger than your faults. God's faithfulness is bigger than your failures. No matter how many failures you've had or disappointments you've experienced, God is the God of second chances, and third and fourth and thousandth. It's never too late to be who you might have been. How has God redeemed the failures in your life and used them for His purposes?

5. In your opinion, what's more amazing: genesis or synaptogenesis? God's ability to create or re-create? And why?

Final Thoughts

The will of God is the glory of God.

Sometimes God chooses to glorify Himself through miracles. Other times, for reasons that are beyond human reason, He chooses not to. But one way or the other, the ultimate goal is not healing. It's God's glory.

Sometimes God is glorified through deliverance that circumvents natural law. Sometimes God is glorified through good old-fashioned perseverance.

During those difficult seasons when God doesn't perform the miracle we've been praying for, we've got to fall back on who we know God to be.

God is good, all the time.
All the time, God is good.

Doubt is putting our circumstances between us and God. *Faith* is putting God between us and our circumstances. The choice is ours.

Reflection Questions

1. In your experience, is it easier to forgive others or forgive yourself? Are there any sins in your life that God has forgiven but you have not?

_____

_____

2. Read the story of Abraham and Sarah in Genesis 21:1–7. Sarah said, "Who would have said to Abraham that Sarah would nurse a baby? Yet I have given Abraham a son in his old age!" Are there any situations in your life where it appears that the natural window of opportunity has closed?

———————————————————

———————————————————

3. When was the last time you thanked God for your eyesight? Take one day to do a little experiment: notice what you're looking at. Study the faces of those you love. Observe the nuances of color and texture. Thank God for the sights you take for granted—like looking at yourself in the mirror.

———————————————————

———————————————————

4. Are there any areas of your life where you need to rebuke helplessness? Is there a temptation you can't overcome? A bad habit you can't seem to break? A bad attitude you can't seem to change? Name it. Rebuke it. Now ask God to help you overcome it by the power of the Holy Spirit.

———————————————————

———————————————————

5. Study the stories referenced in this session:

> Mark 5:24–34
>
> John 4:7–21
>
> Matthew 9:9–13
>
> Mark 1:40–45
>
> John 8:1–11

Where do you find yourself in these stories? How do you think Jesus would respond to you? Write your own story, like the stories recorded in the Gospels.

_____

_____

_____

_____

_____

_____

_____

_____

_____

_____

_____

_____

_____

_____

_____

_____

_____

_____

The Next Step

In his book *You'll Get Through This*, Max Lucado shares the story of his friend JJ Jasper, whose five-year-old son, Cooper, was killed in a dune buggy crash. What started out as a fun father-son outing turned into tragedy when the buggy flipped over.

JJ had to make the toughest call of his life—calling his wife to tell her that their son had died in his arms. Before JJ made the call, the Holy Spirit gave him the words to say, just as He promised He would do during life's most difficult moments. JJ said, "I've got some bad news to share, but before I tell you, I want you to think about everything that you know that is good about God."

Think about everything you know that is good about God.

After witnessing how his friend walked through the valley of the shadow of death, Max decided to do exactly what JJ prescribed. He knew he might need that checklist someday too. So Max quarried the Bible for the goodness of God. Here's the short list he came up with:

> God is still sovereign no matter what. He still knows my name. Angels still respond to his call. The hearts of rulers still bend at his bidding. The death of Jesus still saves souls. The Spirit of God still indwells saints. Heaven is still only heartbeats away. The grave is still temporary housing. God is still faithful. He is not caught off guard. He uses everything for his glory and my ultimate good. He uses tragedy to accomplish his will and his will is right, holy, and perfect. Sorrow may come with the night, but joy comes with the morning.[16]

This week, try coming up with your own list.
Write it down.
If you feel comfortable doing so, share it with the group next week.

The Seventh Sign

One Little Yes

Before watching Session 7,
read chapters 22–25 in *The Grave Robber*.

Read, pray, and meditate on the seventh sign, found in John 11:32–44:

When Mary reached the place where Jesus was and saw him, she fell at his feet and said, "Lord, if you had been here, my brother would not have died."

When Jesus saw her weeping, and the Jews who had come along with her also weeping, he was deeply moved in spirit and troubled. "Where have you laid him?" he asked.

"Come and see, Lord," they replied.

Jesus wept.

Then the Jews said, "See how he loved him!"

But some of them said, "Could not he who opened the eyes of the blind man have kept this man from dying?"

Jesus, once more deeply moved, came to the tomb. It was a cave with a stone laid across the entrance. "Take away the stone," he said.

"But, Lord," said Martha, the sister of the dead man, "by this time there is a bad odor, for he has been there four days."

Then Jesus said, "Did I not tell you that if you believe, you will see the glory of God?"

So they took away the stone. Then Jesus looked up and said, "Father, I thank you that you have heard me. I knew that you always hear me, but I said this for the benefit of the people standing here, that they may believe that you sent me."

When he had said this, Jesus called in a loud voice, "Lazarus, come out!" The dead man came out, his hands and feet wrapped with strips of linen, and a cloth around his face.

Jesus said to them, "Take off the grave clothes and let him go."

Write down your personal reflections.

Introduction

In an interview with *Rolling Stone* magazine, Bono was asked his opinion on Jesus with this question: "Christ has His rank among the world's greatest thinkers. But Son of God, isn't that far-fetched?" The lead singer of U2 and global crusader against poverty responded:

> No, it's not far-fetched to me. Look, the secular response to the Christ story always goes like this. He was a great prophet who had a lot to say along the lines of other great prophets, be they Elijah, Muhammad, Buddha, or Confucius. But actually Christ doesn't allow you that. He doesn't let you off that hook. Christ says, "No. I'm not saying I'm a teacher, don't call me a teacher. I'm not saying I'm a prophet. I'm saying: I'm the Messiah. I'm saying: I am God incarnate." And people say: No, no, please, just be a prophet. A prophet we can take. So what you're left with is either Christ was who He said he was—the Messiah—or a complete nutcase.[17]

While most people have no issue accepting Jesus as a compassionate healer or wise teacher or even a religious prophet, that isn't who He alleged to be. He claimed to be the Son of God. And as C. S. Lewis famously observed, Jesus is either a liar, a lunatic, or in fact who He claimed to be—Lord.[18]

Either Jesus is Lord of all or He's not Lord at all.

So which is it? That one decision will determine your eternal destiny. It will also make the impossible possible!

Video Notes

As you watch the video for this session, use the following space to take notes.

Group Discussion

1. Share one of your most embarrassing moments with the group.

2. Have you ever felt like God was a day late and a dollar short, only to discover that He was right on time? Share that experience with the group.

3. Have you ever put a comma where God put a period or put a period where God put a comma? What is your natural tendency?

4. Have you ever gotten passive-aggressive with God? How have you dealt with those tendencies?

5. Oswald Chambers once said, "Sometimes it looks like God is missing the mark because we're too short-sighted to see what he's aiming for."[19] What do you think God is aiming for?

Final Thoughts

The resurrection isn't something we celebrate one day a year. It's something we celebrate every day in every way. The resurrection of dead bodies is nothing short of miraculous, but the resurrection miracles don't stop there. God raises dreams from the dead. He resurrects dead relationships. And no matter what part of your personality has died at the hands of sin or suffering or Satan himself, the Grave Robber came to give you your life back!

Jesus Christ didn't just die on a cross to make bad people good.
He walked out of the tomb to bring dead people to life!

The resurrection radically redefines reality.
When Jesus walked out of the tomb under His own power, the word *impossible* was removed from our vocabulary.

Nothing is impossible! The resurrection is the history changer, the game changer.

All bets are off.
All bets are on Jesus.

But the trick is learning to live as if Jesus was crucified yesterday, rose from the dead today, and is coming back tomorrow!

Reflection Questions

1. On a scale of 1 to 10, do you have *preventative faith* or *resurrection faith*? Preventative faith believes that God can *keep things from happening*. Resurrection faith believes that God can *reverse the irreversible*.

1	2	3	4	5	6	7	8	9	10
Preventative									Resurrection

2. Romans 10:9 says, "If you confess with your mouth, 'Jesus is Lord,' and believe in your heart that God raised him from the dead, you will be saved." What is the difference between "confessing with your mouth" and "believing in your heart"? Have you done both? Have you confessed your sin and professed your faith in Jesus Christ?

   _____

   _____

3. Oswald Chambers once said, "Sometimes it looks like God is missing the mark because we're too short-sighted to see what he's aiming for."[20] Is it possible that you aren't dreaming big enough? Thinking long enough? Maybe what you think of as the end goal is really just the beginning of something bigger and better. Read, reflect on, and journal on John 1:50: "You will see greater things than that."

_____

_____

4. What is God calling you out of?

_____

_____

5. When Jesus reveals His identity as the resurrection and the life and asks Martha if she believes, Martha says, "Yes, Lord."[21] One little *yes* can change your life! What do you need to say yes to?

_____

_____

The Next Step

After asserting His identity as the resurrection and the life, Jesus popped a point-blank question that punctuated Martha's life: "Do you believe this?"[22] Remember, Jesus hadn't called Lazarus out of the tomb quite yet, so Martha was still in the depths of despair. Hope was four days dead. Yet Martha responded with her simple profession of faith:

Yes, Lord.[23]

One little *yes* can change your life.
One little *yes* can change your eternity.

The litmus test is the same now as it was then. The only question on God's final exam is, *Do you believe this?* It's not a multiple-choice question. It's true or false. And it's the most important question you'll ever answer. That one decision will determine your eternal destiny. The good news is that it's an open-book exam, and God reveals the right answer in Romans 10:9:

If you confess with your mouth, "Jesus is Lord," and believe in your heart that God raised him from the dead, you will be saved.

Have you confessed your sin?
Have you professed your faith in Christ?
If not, why not do it now?
Today can be the first day of the rest of your life.
Today can be the day your impossible becomes possible.
Today can be the day that one little *yes* changes everything.

NOTES

1. I'm indebted to Dorothy L. Sayers for this sentiment from her 1942 essay "Why Work?"

2. The exact quote is, "Every now and then a man's mind is stretched by a new idea or sensation, and never shrinks back to its former dimensions." From Oliver Wendell Holmes, *The Autocrat of the Breakfast-Table* (Boston: James R. Osgood and Co., 1873); online at Project Gutenberg, http://www.gutenberg.org/ebooks/751.

3. John 2:3.

4. See George Dantzig, http://en.wikipedia.org/wiki/George_Dantzig; "The Unsolvable Math Problem," Snopes.com, updated June 28, 2011, http://www.snopes.com/college/homework/unsolvable.asp; and George Dantzig, http://en.wikipedia.org/wiki/George_Dantzig.

5. See Philippians 4:13 ESV.

6. See Ephesians 3:20.

7. See Romans 8:37.

8. See Zechariah 2:8.

9. See Isaiah 62:12.

10. See Romans 8:17.

11. See John 1:12.

12. See Mark Batterson, *The Grave Robber* (Grand Rapids: Baker, 2014), 139; and Deborah A. Small, George Loewenstein, and Paul Slovic, "Sympathy and Callousness: The Impact of Deliberative Thought on Donations to Identifiable and Statistical Victims," *Organizational Behavior and Human Decision Processes* 102, no. 2 (March 2007): 143–53.

13. Bittersweet Creative, "Lily Kate: A Personal Portrait of Hope and Overcoming," *Bittersweet* magazine online, April 9, 2014, http://www.bittersweetzine.com/2014/04/lily-kate-a-personal-portrait-of-hope-and-overcoming/.

14. Mark Nepo, *The Book of Awakening* (San Francisco: Conari, 2000), 131.

15. Albert Einstein, "Religion and Science," *New York Times Magazine*, November 9, 1930, 1–4, http://www.sacred-texts.com/aor/einstein/einsci.htm.

16. Max Lucado, *You'll Get Through This: Hope and Help for Your Turbulent Times* (Nashville: Thomas Nelson, 2013), 28.

17. Michka Assayas, *Bono: In Conversation with Michka Assayas* (New York: Riverhead, 2005), 205.

18. C. S. Lewis, *Mere Christianity* (1952; repr., New York: HarperCollins, 2001), 54.

19. Oswald Chambers, "The Big Compelling of God," in *My Utmost for His Highest*, http://utmost.org/classic/the-big-compelling-of-god-classic/.

20. Ibid.

21. John 11:27.

22. John 11:26.

23. John 11:27.

Mark Batterson is the *New York Times* bestselling author of *The Circle Maker*. The lead pastor of National Community Church in Washington, DC, Mark has a doctor of ministry degree from Regent University and lives on Capitol Hill with his wife, Lora, and their three children.

"Mark reminds us that faith in Jesus is worth the risk."

–MAX LUCADO, pastor and bestselling author

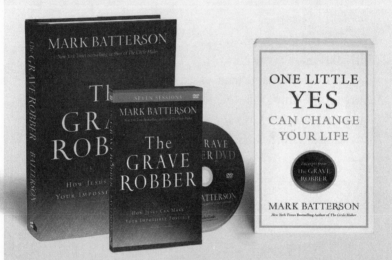

Find resources for individuals and small groups at
www.MarkBatterson.com

🐦 @MarkBatterson

📘 Mark Batterson

📷 @MarkBatterson

Connect with National Community Church at
www.TheatreChurch.com

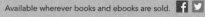